*Les Murray*

# TALLER WHEN PRONE

Les Murray is the author of many books of poetry. His collection *Subhuman Redneck Poems* received the T. S. Eliot Prize in 1996, and in 1998 he was awarded the Queen's Gold Medal for Poetry, presented by Queen Elizabeth II. He lives in New South Wales, Australia.

# ALSO BY LES MURRAY

*The Vernacular Republic: Selected Poems*

*The Daylight Moon and Other Poems*

*The Rabbiter's Bounty: Collected Poems*

*The Boys Who Stole the Funeral: A Novel Sequence*

*Dog Fox Field*

*Translations from the Natural World*

*Subhuman Redneck Poems*

*Fredy Neptune: A Novel in Verse*

*Learning Human: Selected Poems*

*Conscious and Verbal*

*Poems the Size of Photographs*

*The Biplane Houses*

# TALLER WHEN PRONE

— POEMS —

# Les Murray

*Farrar, Straus and Giroux*
*New York*

Farrar, Straus and Giroux
18 West 18th Street, New York 10011

Copyright © 2010 by Les Murray
Distributed in Canada by D&M Publishers, Inc.
Printed in the United States of America
Originally published in 2010 by Black Inc., Australia
Published in the United States in 2011 by Farrar, Straus and Giroux
First American paperback edition, 2012

The Library of Congress has cataloged the hardcover edition as follows:
Murray, Les A., 1938–
    Taller when prone : poems / Les Murray. — 1st American ed.
        p.    cm.
    ISBN 978-0-374-27237-1 (alk. paper)
    I. Title.

PR9619.3.M83T35 2011
821'.912—dc22

                                        2010033150

Paperback ISBN: 978-0-374-53308-3

Designed by Thomas Deverall

www.fsgbooks.com

1    3    5    7    9    10    8    6    4    2

*To the glory of God*

# Contents

*Taller When Prone*

# From a Tourist Journal

In a precinct of liver stone, high
on its dais, the Taj seems bloc hail.

We came to Agra over honking roads
being built under us, past baby wheat
and undoomed beasts and walking people.
Lorries shouldered white marble loads.

Glamour of ads demeaned street life
in the city; many buildings were
held aloft with liverwurst mortar.
I have not left the Taj Mahal.

Camels were lozenge-clipped like rug pile
and workhorses had kept their stallionhood
even in town, around the Taj wall.
Anglos deny theirs all Bollywood.

On Indian streets, tourists must still
say too much no, and be diminished.
Pedlars speak of it to their lit thumbs.
I have not left the Taj Mahal.

Poor men, though, in Raj-time uniforms:
I'd felt that lure too, and understood.
In Delhi, we craned up at a sky-high
sandstone broom cinched with balustrades.

Schoolkids from Nagaland posed with us
below it, for their brag books, and new cars
streamed left and right to the new world,
but from Agra Fort we'd viewed, through haze,

perfection as a factory making depth,
pearl chimneys of the Taj Mahal.

## Bluelookout Mountain

Bluelookout is a tractor climb
to where you see the South Pacific.
The animals who stay
up there don't know to see it.

Bluelookout is the colours and smooth
texture of forest pigeons
though it's 'dirty' in some folds
with scrub the old ones would have burnt.

Grasses of exotic green
radiate down its ridge lines
just how snow would lie

and the owner's house snuggles
in close, not for shelter
but out of all the view.

*Note: the spelling Bluelookout as one word with the accent
on the first syllable reflects local pronunciation.*

## The Sharman Drum

What year was the very best Mallee Show?
When Lord Hopetoun attended, that bottled year?
When Skuthorpe danced his horse for some peer,
Lord Brassicae? Or was it Brassey?
and Sunshine harvesters turned into Massey –
No no, what year? I need to hear.
When the Wallup Pipe Band piped music and rum
and Jim Sharman's pugs beat the step-up drum
and ladies dressed up their skills and tone
or dressed for each other, or themselves alone,
when the ticket strung through the tweedy eye
of each member's lapel meant pedigree –
What year, what year? It was every year
after the last. They made a past,
the ring events, the Wyandotte hens
the marble cakes in their ribboned pens.
What year was the greatest Mallee Show?
When Warracknabeal yachts sailed on Lake Glue,
bagging needles flew and girth straps strained.
The best show was any year it rained!

## The Toppled Head

A big bald head is asleep
like Lenin on a pavement.
Tipping backward, it starts
a great mouth-breathing snore
throttling as stormwater,
loud as a hangar door
    running on rails
but his companion gently
reshapes his pillow, till his
position's once more foetal,
breathing toward his feet.
His timbre goes silent, and
the glottal dies in a gulp.

# Definitions

Effete: a pose
of palace cavalry officers
in plum Crimean fig,
spurs and pointed boots,

not at all the stamp
of tight-buttoned guards
executing arm-geometry
in the shouting yards,

but sitting his vehicle
listening to tanks change gears
amid oncoming fusiliers
one murmurs the style

that has carried his cohort
to this day, and now will test them:
*You have to kill them, Giles,*
*You can't arrest them.*

# The Conversations

A full moon always rises at sunset
and a person is taller at night.
Many fear their phobias more than death.
The glass King of France feared he'd shatter.
Chinese eunuchs kept their testes in spirit.

Your brain can bleed from a sneeze-breath.
A full moon always rises at sunset
and a person is taller when prone.
Donald Duck was once banned in Finland
because he didn't wear trousers,

his loins were feather-girt like Daisy's
but no ostrich hides its head in sand.
The cure for scurvy was found
then long lost through medical theory.
The Beginning is a steady white sound.

The full moon rises at sunset
and lemurs and capuchin monkeys
pass a millipede round to get off on
its powerful secretions. Mouthing it
they wriggle in bliss on the ground.

The heart of a groomed horse slows down.
A fact is a small compact faith,
a sense-datum to beasts, a power to man
even if true, even while true –
we read these laws in Isaac Neurone.

One woman had sixty-nine children.
Some lions mate fifty times a day.
Napoleon had a victory addiction.
A full moon always rises at sunset.
Soldiers now can get in the family way.

## The Double Diamond

He was the family soldier,
deadly marksman on tropic steeps.

Home, he spurned the drunk heir-splitting
of working for parents, and stayed poor

on share farm after fence-sagging share farm.
Goodbye! yelled the kids to new friends.

Slim sang his songs, and his kind
wife's skin was sensitive to gossip.

Over eighty, he stands in his suit
outside where she, quick-spoken Alice

lies tight-packed in varnished timber.
As the family gather, he tells me

*Late years, I've lived at the hospital.*
*Now I'll forget the way there.*

## As Country Was Slow

*for Peter*

Our new motorway
is a cross-country fort
and we reinforcements
speed between earthworks
water-sumps and counterscarps,
breaking out on wide glimpses,
flying the overpasses –

Little paper lanterns
march up and down dirt,
wrapped round three chopsticks
plastic shrub-guards grow bushes
to screen the real bush,
to hide the old towns
behind sound-walls and green –

Wildlife crossings underneath
the superglued pavement
are jeep size; beasts must see
nature restart beyond.
The roads are our nature
shining beyond delay,
fretting to race on –

Any check in high speed
can bleed into gravel
and hang pastel wreaths
over roadside crosses.
Have you had your scare yet? –
It made you a driver
not an ever-young name.

We're one Ireland, plus
at least six Great Britains
welded around Mars
and cross-linked by cars –
Benzene, diesel, autobahn:
they're a German creation,
these private world-splicers.

The uncle who farmed our place
was an Arab of his day
growing fuel for the horses
who hauled the roads then.
1914 ended that. Will I
see fuel crops come again?
I'll ride a slow vehicle

before cars are slow
as country was slow.

# The Death of Isaac Nathan, 1864

Stone statues of ancient waves
tongue like dingoes on shore
in time with wave-glitter on the harbour
but the shake-a-leg chants of the Eora

are rarely heard there any more
and the white man who drew their nasals
as footprints on five-lined paper
lies flat away up Pitt Street,

lies askew on gravel Pitt Street.
Jumping off startled horses come men
and other men down off the horse-tram
which ladies stay aboard and cram

their knuckles in their teeth, because a
grandson of the last king of Poland
is lying behind the rear wheels,
lying in his blood and his music sheets

where he missed his step and fell
to be Sydney tramways' first victim.
Byron's Hebrew melodist, driven
out of London by Lord Melbourne,

by the inked horns of Lord Melbourne,
is now being lifted tenderly,
he, the Anglican who used
to pray wrapped in a white shawl

is being wrapped in a tarpaulin
and carried in catch-up cadence
with crotchets he might have scored,
carried over streets to his residence

to lie in state on his table:
Our Father and Melech ha-olam,
then to go in a bourdon to Newtown
and sleep near the real Miss Havisham.

## The Filo Soles

When tar roads came
in the barefoot age
crossing them was hell
with the sun at full rage.
Kids learned to dip
their feet in the black
and quench with dust,
dip again, and back
in the dust, to form
a dark layered crust
and carry quick soles
over the worst
annealing their leather
though many splash scornfully
across, to flayed ground.

*Midi*

Muscles and torsoes of cloud
ascended over the mountains.
The fields looked like high speed
so new-mown was the hay,

then the dark blue Italian lavender
met overhead, a strange maize
deeply planted as mass javelins
in the hoed floor of the land.

Insects in plastic armour stared
from their turrets, and munched
as others machined stiffly over us
and we turned, enchanted
in sweet walling breath
under far-up gables of the lavender.

## Observing the Mute Cat

Clean water in the house
but the cat laps up clay water
outside. Drinking the earth.

His pile, being perfect,
ignores the misting rain.

A charcoal Russian
he opens his mouth like other cats
and mimes a greeting mew.

At one bound top-speed across
the lawn and halfway up
the zippy pear tree. Why? Branches?
Stopping puzzles him.

Eloquent of purr
or indignant tail
he politely hates to be picked up.
His human friend never does it.

He finds a voice
in the flyscreen, rattling it,
hanging cruciform on it,
all to be let in
to walk on his man.

He can fish food pellets
out of the dispenser, but waits,
preferring to be served.

A mouse he was playing
on the grass ran in under him.
Disconsolate, at last he wandered
off – and drew and fired
himself in one motion.

He is often above you
and appears where you will go.

He swallows his scent, and
discreet with his few stained birds
he carries them off to read.

## Buttress on a High Cutting

Angophora, rusty-shelled
tree without a deep hold
but when its hill split,
this side root, jutting
out into sun glare
              bent
and flowed down, tight
as mailbag wax, rain
year by drought year
to the new ground level
buttressing its trunk still
in high bush overhead
              far
above blue roadbed
and palm-tree eruptions,
this pirouette of wood-
coated trouserleg, taller
than its many-buckled man.

# Ovoids

Moist black as sago pearls
in white Chinese tea
heads of women lovingly
watch babies grabbing
like unsteady moons
in a wading pool full
of cherry balloons.
Cushions and knees
and round toes in grass
under tropic leaves
the scented sweet
skin glazed in sweat –
all snapped from above in
the aqueous ovarian.

## Nursing Home

*Ne tibi supersis*:
don't outlive yourself,
panic, or break a hip
or spit purée at the staff
at the end of gender,
never a happy ender –

yet in the pastel light
of indoors, there is a lady
who has distilled to love
beyond the fall of memory.

She sits holding hands
with an ancient woman
who calls her *brother* and *George*
as bees summarise the garden.

## Fame

We were at dinner in Soho
and the couple at the next table
rose to go. The woman paused to say
to me: *I just wanted you to know*
*I have got all your cook books*
*and I swear by them!*

    I managed
to answer her: *Ma'am*
*they've done you nothing but good!*
which was perhaps immodest
of whoever I am.

## Cattle-Hoof Hardpan

Trees from modern times don't bear
but the old China pear
still standing in the soil
of 1880 rains fruit.

## Phone Canvass

Chatting, after the donation part,
the Blind Society's caller
answered my shy questions:

'. . . and I love it on the street,
all the echo and air pressure,
people in my forehead and
metal stone brick, the buildings
passing in one side of my head . . .

I can hear you smiling.'

## King Lear Had Alzheimer's

The great feral novel
every human is in
is ruthless. It exists
to involve and deflate.
It is the meek talking.

The great feral novel
is published, not written
(science bits may be written).
Media grope in its shallows.
The Real Story is their owners.

The feral novel can get you
told the lies about you,
let you hear the Line about you.
It may even tell the truth
if truth is the cool story.

Any farmer who breaks
and suicides, some lot's
politicians wanted him
o don't say dead. Gone.
Dead doesn't always die.

The folk novel's eyes
did register the barbed wire
and how to get behind it.
Being in the novel helped
a lot in, it says. Some out.

A father jealous of one son's
bush skills failed to prove
himself the better man, and caused
a younger son's death trying.
When the skilled son complained

at being kept dependent
and dirt poor for punishment
only others listened
and others don't back you
in plots not their own.

In theirs, they may be hero
even to acquaintances
but then if they rise
into notice, into print,
fellow convicts eye them.

*The man next door*
*cursed our builders' noise.*
*He was writing a book,*
*so we scoffed, through the hedge,*
*Shops would sell him a book!*

The great feral novel
heaped up streetsful of flowers
for the faux-demure princess
then sniggered them away.
What survives survives this.

## Science Fiction

I can travel
faster than light
so can you
the speed of thought
the only trouble
is at destinations
our thought balloons
are coated invisible
no one there sees us
and we can't get out
to be real or present
phone and videophone
are almost worse
we don't see a journey
but stay in our space
just talking and joking
with those we reach
but can never touch
the nothing that can hurt us
how lovely and terrible
and lonely is this.

## Atlantic Pavements

In Rio, cobalt peaks wore
ochre suburbs and children
and stair-stepping samba
convoyed tipped nudes down.

In Lisbon, a singer
acknowledged (obrigada!)
coins plinked on the dado
(obrigada!) of her fado:

from no love again
men trailed back to ships
and the ropes they wing-walked
made a vast wind-lobed brain.

Black, chipper and white
street mosaics of Lisbon,
pavement-scrolls of Rio,
    sargasso between.

# Refusing Saul's Armour

*i.m. Lex Banning, poet, 1921–65*

x times y marks the spot
where my maths hit the wall.
It was all x from there.
In my last school exam
I drew maths on the paper.

Degrees were critique
but my mind was a groover
and a fiver a week
postponed me as a lover.
That, and sexual catastrophe

my parents had taught me
in their innocent mating
so I read unset books
slept in buildings and long grass
years before the Haight

I mean the Haight Ashbury
while faith, faith and tobacco
kept the Black Dog at bay.
When all turned to hope and blame
was his teeth-baring day.

# Our Dip in the Rift Valley

*for Lasse Söderberg*

We never heard what my mate heard
descending to the Dead Sea by bus:
a jet fighter far below him
streaking north Gomorrah and SDOM!
Our trip was nearly in peacetime.
I remember my surprise

at my first view of our goal,
not a white brine pan,
it twinkled cheerfully blue
like any sunny lake.
It wasn't grey, or gelid.

I remember the stumps of pale
earth at the stop going down,
how I introduced the haughty
Russian lady to one: *Mrs Rein,
meet Mrs Lot.* The smile this got.

I recall us in our pallor
at the stand-offish kibbutz
on its narrow shelf of shore
past the Qumran scroll mines,
how they had fresh water
hoses afloat on the surface

to wash our mouths and eyes
if the clear Mars-gravity water
got into them, as we drifted
high as triremes. The appalling
caustic and thistlehead bite of it.

I'd forgotten the black mud
under water, but the natron
stench returns, and nearly refreshes!
Thanks for that day, from back
when an orange cost one shekel.

# Brown Suits

Sorting clothes for movie costume,
chocolate suits of bull-market cut,
slim blade ties ending in fringes,
brimmed felt hats, and the sideburned
pork-pie ones that served them. I lived then.

The right grade of suit coat, unbuttoned
can still get you a begrudged free meal
in a café. But seat sweat off sunned vinyl,
ghostly through many dry-cleans
and the first deodorants. I lived then

and worked for the man who abolished
bastards. The prime minister* who
said on air *I'm what you call a bastard.
Illegitimate.* And drove a last stake
through that lousiest distinction.

*Prime Minister J. G. Gorton (1968–71)*

# Southern Hemisphere Garden

This autumn grove, in the half world
that has no fall season, shows a mauve
haze all through its twig-sheaves
and over a rich spangled ground
of Persian leaves.
      Inroads of sun
are razzle gold and textile blond
out to the greens and blady-grass baulks
mown in drought along the pond.
      Thoth
the many ibis lift for the night perches,
the nankeen heron has moved to Japan
but ink-blue waterhens preen long feet
or, flashing undertail
like feathers of the queen protea, run
each other round the brimming rain dam
whose inner sky is black below shine
as if Space were closer, down.
      Back this summer
of the out-of-season Christmas snow
that scotched the bushfires in Victoria
I was out under green leaf-tressed
deciduous, hooking a pole saw
high and snapping down water-stressed
abortive limbs from beneath China
and Europe and America.

Now lichens up
the yeast boughs of those trees are bazaar
trinkets on the belly-dance troupe
at the rural show, who circled sidestepping
to the tappets of a drum.
          'Sacred women's business,'
they laughed after, adjusting coins
over their floured and bake-oil skins,
strolling, antique, unaccusingly bizarre.

## The Suspect Corpse

The dead man lay, nibbled, between
dark carriages of a rocky river,

a curled load of himself, in cheap
clothes crusted in dried water.

Noisy awe, nose-crimped, sent us up the
gorge, to jail, in case we were hoaxing.

Following us back down next morning
forensics mentioned his wish bone

but never could pry any
names from between his teeth,

not his own, nor who had lashed
his ankles, or put boulders in his clothes.

After three months, he could only
generalise, and had started smiling.

## Eucalypts in Exile

They've had so many jobs:
boiling African porridge. Being printed on.
Sopping up malaria. Flying in Paris uprisings.
Supporting a stork's nest in Spain.

Their suits are neater abroad,
of denser drape, un-nibbled:
they've left their parasites at home.

They flower out of bullets
and, without any taproot,
draw water from way deep.
Blown down in high winds
they reveal the black sun of that trick.

Standing around among shed limbs
and loose craquelure of bark
is home-country stuff
but fire is ingrained.
They explode the mansions of Malibu
because to be eucalypts
they have to shower sometimes in Hell.

Their humans, meeting them abroad,
often grab and sniff their hands.

Loveable singly or unmarshalled
they are merciless in a gang.

## The Monroe Survey

Moss carpet coherent over
a worldwide swamp sea,
carmine, olive, blood.

Rare mountains, stepped back
like pipe organs amid an infinite crowd
or abrupt as trucks.

A few are hot-water volcanoes.
Gut-coloured vast tube life-forms
sup their overflow as it streams down.

Breathable air. No night.
No atmospheric weather.
The ground sways as you walk

but you can sleep dry on it
and slice the upper rind like felt
to fold back and get some darkness.

You can eat the knobby vegetal layer
the whole pelt floats on.
It tastes like mushrooms, or bok choy.

Planet Monroe. *Moine rua*, red bog
as we have named it. Inconvenient, benign,
useless for forced landings.

For a while, after humans came,
it would resist, and make poignant
the little suicide of emigration.

# Reading by Starlight

Respite. Awe.
Proof we are awake:

the galaxy, streamed like sugarbag
in a char branch
fronted by chinning bees.

The illuminant immense
irrefutable by science.

The past at all its depths,
dream countries for surplus people.

Campfires of the once vivid.

No one solid, feeding their bones
to null gravity, has travelled
one light-minute in the rocket age

but Astaire globes on out
into brown light, toward Betelgeuse
with no rattle from his tap-shoes.

Drips of light speeding earthward.

Tonight, sane people will be whaled
aloft by aliens, for science,
and returned uneaten.

Capstans of roped pearl
each seed a junction of forces
and nearer gunshots over all
flame, snowflake, syrup, rose –

Mortals voyage there out-of-body
and return as fiction
or numbers, over the thin

sky-bridges of Metropolis
down through satellite levels
to feed the new human force

made of meaning and breakthrough
required by careers.

## Cherries from Young

Cherries from Young
that pretty town,
white cherries and black,
sun-windows on them.

Cherries from Young
the tastiest ever
grow in drought time
on farms above there.

One lip-teased drupe
or whole sweet gallop
poured out of cardboard
in whatever year,

cherries from Young.
All the roads back
go down into Young
that early town.

## Lunar Eclipse

Many birds were making outcry
at the rotting Satsuma-plum moon
rising above the ocean cliffs
stacked high as a British address.
Moon was queer, too, a burnt-sugar
apparition with clouds of its own
darkening its face above the city
but then two Tongan bouncers
from the club found the word:
*foi'atelolo*, a baked pig's liver
fat with oil, a chief's portion
or praise-name for a pretty woman –
At that, the round man of the sky
began to reveal his gold edge.

## Croc

This police car with a checkered seam
of blue and white teeth along its side
lies in cover like a long-jawed
flat dog beside the traffic stream.

# High-speed Bird

At full tilt, air gleamed –
and a window-struck kingfisher,
snatched up, lay on my palm
still beating faintly.

Slowly, a tincture
of whatever consciousness is
infused its tremor, and
ram beak wide as scissors

all hurt loganberry inside,
it crept over my knuckle
and took my outstretched finger
in its wire foot-rings.

Cobalt wings, shutting on beige
body. Gold under-eye whiskers,
beak closing in recovery
it faced outward from me.

For maybe twenty minutes
we sat together, one on one,
as if staring back or
forward into prehistory.

# The Cowladder Stanzas

Not from a weather direction
black cockatoos come crying over
unflapping as Blériot monoplanes
to crash in pine tops for the cones.

Young dogs, neighbours' dogs
across the creek, bark, chained
off the cows, choked off play, bark
untiring as a nightsick baby, yap
milking times to dark, plead,
ute-dancing dope-eye dogs.

Red-hot pokers up and out
of their tussock. Kniphofia flowers
overlapping many scarlet jubes
form rockets on a stick.
Ignition's mimed by yellow petticoats.

Like all its kind
Python has a hare lip
through which it aims its tongue
at eye-bursting Hare.

Thinking up names
for a lofty farm: High Wallet,
Cow Terraces, Fogsheep,
Rainside, Helmet Brush,
Tipcamber, Dingo Leap.

My boyhood farm cousin spoke
French, and I understood fluently
but not in this world.
It happened just one time
in my early urban sleep.

I know – as they may prefer –
little of the beekeeper family
who've lived for years inside
tall kindling of their forest
in old car bodies, sheds
and the rotted like sailcloth
of their first shore day.

And the blue wonga pigeon
walks under garden trees
and pumpkins lean like wheels
out of their nurturing trash.

We climbed the Kokoda Track.
Goura pigeon, rain, kau kau.
Dad said after the war
they wanted soldier settlement
blocks in New Guinea. This was struck
down by a minister named Hasluck.
Paul Hasluck. Dad's grateful now:
it would have been bloody Mau Mau.

## The Farm Terraces

Beautiful merciless work
around the slopes of earth
terraces cut by curt hoe
at the orders of hunger
or a pointing lord.
Levels eyed up to rhyme
copied from grazing animals
round the steeps of earth,
balconies filtering water
down stage to stage of drop.
Wind-stirred colours of crop
swell between walked bunds
miles of grass-rimmed contour
harvests down from the top
by hands long in the earth.
Baskets of rich made soil
boosted up poor by the poor,
ladder by freestone prop
stanzas of chant-long lines
by backwrenching slog, before
money, gave food and drunk
but rip now like slatted sails
(some always did damn do)
down the abrupts of earth.

## The Drizzle of Chefs' Knives

Such a lot sailing north:
coal, the Blue Mountains,
farm projects, cutthroat sheep,
winter whales hoisting breath.

Our other coasts look out
on deepwater views
but north fronts the Islands
the ocean of prahus.

Talk too wet to suit the dry
sing too dry to move the wet –
when I was small it was soldiers
drinking north to face gunshot.

On frosty nights, crossing
that hairy lizard the Inland
you could burn a bed of sticks
and sleep above it on sand

and up north they spoke Pidgin
(once English was a pidgin)
but cuisines replaced empires
all across the region.

Croc-shooting hell-for-leather
tamed to a tourist park
and new money bought up culture:
Ishihara dots and *rrark*.

Chefs' knives peeled green islands
as the climate turned bohemian
over Woop Woop of the wind farms
and the bloodshot television.

All of English was once forest
but it sailed to the lagoons.
Now our southern bush needs pipeline
to drink from the monsoons.

# The Sphere

She is delighted afresh
every dawn, to unlid
perfect nothing. That sphere

which extends from the blue
beneath her lashes
clear out to the horizons

of the detail-balloon
that contains all the air.
Blues she sang for years

through colour washes
are gone with the thickening
glasses that narrowed reading

and blind-girl craft work,
the contacts that sucked, bleeding.
Since technology got up

off a Red conveyor,
razored an aqueous ring
and, lasing a layer,

skimmed all that history
off her inner sky,
side clouds have vanished.

She needn't stand demurely
fuming, among ignorers.
Now she rises to her character.

## The Submerged Chute of Bass Strait

Undersea waterfall,
no shoaling slants above,
nowhere a roaring wall.

On all the width of sailing
above the hunters' savannah
sunk by ice-melt, in an event
long ago of seepages, then current,
whitecaps now blow open slather.

Lives and leavings sink
to the drowned cliff knee
and missile down its energy

all along the bloom below,
scrolling the wrestle of directions
that makes the oceans go.

# Visiting Geneva

I came to Geneva
by the bullet train,
up from church kero lamps –
it must have been the bullet train.

I rolled in on a Sunday
to that jewelled circling city
and everything was closed
in the old-fashioned way.

In the city of Palais
and moored Secretariat
I arrived in spring when
the Ferraris come out.

Geneva, refuge of the Huguenots,
Courtauld, Pierrepoint, Haszard,
Boers Joubert and Marais,
Brunel's young Isambard

and John Calvin, unforgiver
in your Taliban hat,
you pervade bare St Peter's
in la France protestante,

Calvin, padlock of the sabbath,
your followers now protect you:
predestination wasn't yours, they claim,
nor were the Elect you,

but: when you were God
sermons went on all day
without numen or presence.
Children were denied play.

I had fun with your moral snobbery
but your great work's your recruits,
your Winners and Losers. You
turned mankind into suits –

and many denims, messer John.

## The Bronze Bull

Went down to Wall Street
and the Bull it was gone
the mighty bronze one
squat lord of Wall Street.
A year and a half
before the subprime
not even a calf
wore bronze on that small street,

some skyscrapers may have.
Squared flow-lines, tight-packed,
are the charging Bull's style.
In battle with his Squaremacht
the dumpy brown Allies
were brave in round turrets
or ice-shaggy as the Bear
but they took home Bull's power.

Haven't been back
among Wall Street diviners
where the long green's assigned its
hourly valuations.
Don't know if the hoof-scraping
humpmaster of freedom
is back in place there
or off fighting Baby Bear.

# Port Jackson Greaseproof Rose

Which spawned more civilisations,
yellow grass or green?

Who made poverty legal?
Who made poverty at all?

Eating a cold pork sandwich
out of greaseproof paper
as I cross to Circular Quay
where the world-ships landed poverty
on the last human continent
where it had not been known.

Linked men straddling their chains
being laughed at by naked people.

This belongs to my midlife:
out of my then suburban city
rise towers of two main kinds,
new glass ones keyed high to catch money
and brown steeples to forgive the poor

who made poverty illegal
and were sentenced here for it.

And the first jumbo jets descend
like mates whose names you won't recall,
going down behind the city.

This midlife white timber ferry
scatters curly bohemian glass
one molecule thick, to float above

green dark of laws older than poverty
and I hold aloft my greaseproof rose.

## The Springfields

Lead drips out of
a burning farm rail.
Their Civil War.

# Rugby Wheels

*i.m. Matt Laffan 1970–2009*

Four villages in Ireland
knew never to mix their blood
but such lore gets lost
in the emigrations.
Matt Laffan's parents learned it
in their marriage of genes

they could never share again.
They raised Matt through captaincies
and law degrees. And he exalted them
with his verve and clarities,
sat on a rugby tribunal,
drank beers a third his height

and rode a powered wheelchair
akimbo as in a chariot
with tie-clip, combed red hair,
causes to plead. Beloved in Sydney
he created a travel website
for the lame, and grinned among them

*Doors will often open.*
*Beware a step or two*
*down or up when they do,*
and he told self-doubters
*You'll always be taller than me!*
as he flew his electoral box-kite.

Popular with women, and yet
vision of him in their company
often shows a precipice near
or a balcony-lit corridor.
I would have lacked his
heroism in being a hero.

# A Frequent Flyer Proposes a Name

Sexburga Drive is a steep mud lane
but Sexburga, she was Queen of Kent
fourteen centuries ago.
She tried to rule as well as reign
but her tough spear-thanes grated No!
she's but a wife-man, a loaf-kneader:
we will not obey a bodice-feeder.
No precedent, said Witan. Quite unkent
so on Sheppey isle she built a convent.

But now, in an era more Amazon,
the notion has come to the jarl of London,
white-polled Boris, to move Heathrow
east to the marshy Thames outflow
so jetliners may leave their keening cry
out over the Channel and grim North Sea –
and Celtic queens have ruled: Boudicca, Bess,
but your Saxon ones still await redress
so savour this name: London Sexburga Airport.

## Hesiod on Bushfire

Poxes of the Sun or of the mind
bring the force-ten firestorms.
After come same-surname funerals,
junked theory, praise of mateship.

Love the gum forest, camp out in it
but death hosts your living in it, brother.
You need buried space
and cellars have a convict foetor:

only pubs kept them. Houses shook them off
wherever Diggers moved to.
Only opal desert digs homes by dozer,
the cool Hobbit answer.

Cellars, or bunkers, mustn't sit square
under the fuel your blazing house will be,
but nearby, roofed refractory,
tight against igniting air-miles.

Power should come underground
from Fortress Suburbia, and your treasures
stay back there, where few now
grow up in the fear of grass.

Never build on a summit or a gully top:
fire's an uphill racer deliriously welcomed
by growth it cures of growth.
Shun a ridgeline, window puncher at a thousand degrees.

Sex is Fire, in the ancient Law.
Investment is Fire. Grazing beasts are cool Fire
backburning paddocks to the door.
Ideology is Fire.

The British Isles and giant fig trees are Water.
Horse-penis helicopters are watery TV
but unblocked roads and straight volunteers
are lifesaving spume spray.

Water and Fire chase each other in jet
planes. May you never flee through them
at a generation's end, as when
the Great Depression died, or Marvellous Melbourne.

# The Blame

*for Clare*

Archie was a gun to shoot at biplanes
and an uncle I missed meeting, a dancing whiz
till we lost the footwork that was his.

His elder brother was a timbercutter
who scorned to harvest a rotting tree
so their father wheedled hapless Archie

who felled it crooked, into his brain.
All would rather he had left children
on earth than the mighty grief that followed.

His mother had seen the head-splash happen
five hours before it did, and rode
searching the bush to find the men.

She saw because she knew her world.
Later she would ask her husband
Did you even take your own axe, Allan?

The expert brother got a family block
with a weatherproof dairy and bung clock.
Everything else let the wind through.

Neither he nor his father believed in accident.
Punishment was happening. He was charged rent
to preclude any loans for farm improvement

and eight years' back pay would never come.
Face and bequests were the family-labour system
and his brother's name cried out in dreams.

He, the blamed son, loved all his mother gave him,
the gold watch, touring car, touch of fey;
the latter two failed on his wife's death day

but the car was kept till it fell apart.
Archie's name was shunned, its luck was bad,
but all his survivors got the farm we'd had.

Now nearly everyone who knew an Archie
has rejoined him in more than memory.
Freed of blood, the name starts to return.

# Singing Tour in Vietnam

*for Little Pattie*

Mrs Amp., it's good to meet you.
Hey, did they ever give you
a medal for Long Tan?

No! They reckoned I caused it . . .

(Prone, terrified, while an airliner
crashing in the rubber plantation
got ripped apart. All night.)

## Midwinter Kangaroo Nests

Rasp and whistle
remix this long grass
grown out of hoofprints
to the borders of shade.

The caked white bling
of frost salts melting
tiny birds arrive
sorting for proteins.

As day dries, sleep-tubs
flattened down in the billows
of string-coloured cursive
display no dungs,

not black cattle-green,
not papery human
and quail-run stems revive
lifting longshank fiddlers.

Breath-chaff gets coughed
and dog-drowners tall as khaki
rise in forest that has been
sky-suspended all day.

# The 41st Year of 1968

*i.m. 173 dead in the Victorian fires of 2009*

Hippies always sought rainforest
and they'd used it to wrest
the image of Nature off rednecks
and power off the rest

and Australians had made real progress
though some still had to be
threatened with the law when they wanted
to remove a native tree.

Settler-style clear felling must stay gone
despite what hill-country gumtrees
wreak on settlements at least one summer
in every human generation

so families were burned alive
along steep narrow roads
strung high on the mountains
through spindly second growth.

In deep 1968, one then
simply changed the subject.

## Daylight Cloth

September morning. White is salient.
The unfocussed wet hover of dawn
has cleared the treetops. In high bush
the ski season packs up, tent by tent,

and the Cherokee rose, its new seams
hitched up rather than pruned,
overlaps its live willow easel,
a daylight cloth pelted in white creams.

Minute blossoms of fruit
emerge from lichen's brown wheeze
that has gathered in their trees.
Burnt-off paddocks have gone out

and the sky is bluer for it.
Beyond the sea coast, rebirthed
four-wheel drives tilt, below,
on the tail ends of big seas.

# The Mirrorball

Half a day's drive from Melbourne
until we reach the first town
that's not bypassed by expressway.
Holbrook, once Germantown,
Holbrook of the submarines,
conning tower and periscopes
rising out of sheep land.

It recalls the country towns
up the roads of 1940
each with its trees and Soldier,
its live and dead shop windows
and a story like Les Boyce
we heard about up home,
Taree's Lord Mayor of London.

But now song and story are pixels
of a mirrorball that spins celebrities
in patter and tiny music
so when the bus driver restarts
his vast tremolo of glances
half his earplugged sitters wear
the look of deserted towns.

# Infinite Anthology

Gross motor – co-ordination as a whistle subject
audiation – daydreaming in tunes
papped – snapped by paparazzi
whipping side – right hand side of a convict or sheep
hepcat, hip (from Wolof *hipi-kat*, one who knows the score) –
    spirit in which modernist art goes slumming
instant – (Australian) Nescafé
ranga – redhead

*Creators of single words or phrases are by far the largest class
of poets. Many ignore all other poetry.*

Jail tats – totemic underskin writing done because illegal
lundy – a turned Ulster
rebuttal tapes – counter-propaganda filmed by warplanes
free traders – (19th and early 20th cent.) split bloomers worn
    under voluminous skirts
daylight – second placegetter when winner is very superior
    to field
window licker – a voyeur
fibro – resident of a poorer suburb

*Single-word poets hope to be published and credited in the
Great Book of Anon, the dictionary. The cleverest make their
names serve this purpose: Maxim, Maxim's, Churchillian.*

Irishtown – a Soweto of old-time Catholic labour
bunny boiler – one who kills her offspring
dandruff acting – the stiffest kind of Thespian art

blackout – Aboriginal party or picnic, whites not invited
butternut – homespun cloth dyed with hickory juice
shart – a non-dry fart
Baptist Boilermaker – coffee and soda (an imagined Puritan
    cocktail)

*Single-word poets recycle words in advance of need, or leave
them exposed to the weather of real difference.*

Wedge – cloth bunched in the groin; may cause camel toe
    (q.v.)
wedge – to force the pace or direction
bushed – lost (Australian)
bushed – tired (American)
bushed – suffering camp fever (Canadian)
limo – limousin cattle
proud – castrated but still interested

*Individual words, with their trains of definition loosening
around them, allow us to visit the oracular and sense its
renewing dance.*

Drummy – echoing, hollow-sounding (mining term)
rosebud – American Civil War wound
Shabos goy – Gentile who does small jobs for Orthodox
    Jews on Sabbath or other holy days
choke – to strap loose freight tightly together for transport
off book – (theatre) having one's lines down pat
bugle driver – attachment on a drill to intensify its power in
    sinking screws
tipping elbow – (Aboriginal) sneaking glances at one's watch

## At the Opera

Twitching the curtain aside
reveals an ebullition of talk
including the word *lorgnette*
which I thought
had faded before I was born yet.

# The Relative Gold

Most white people had no relations,
some had things to live up or live down.
In the days of Black Tommy McPherson
the country was more like the town.

Black Tom was a sport in New England
with his red Spanish boots and his sash
but among those who have no relations
respect is called credit. Bare cash

will get us supplies and survival
depending what stories are told,
so Black Tommy reached into New England
and drew out alluvial gold.

Places lightning had shattered in water
and still winked among pebbles were the source
of his drinking with duffers and teamsters.
All this drew the blue Police Force

who badgered him under suspicion
and questioned him where his claim lay
but the claims he half made and grinned off
truly tangled their snarling assay.

*Tom's one of the Tableland's richest men,*
smiled gold buyer Henry Grob,
and some drinker, perhaps a Darwin reader,
took a small packet out of their fob.

The spiked drink that sent Tommy reeling
across the dray road to fall down
gave him visions of two troopers gloating
*You look a real black now, you clown!*

Tom McPherson was never seen working;
he rode a high horse like a lord,
so the police who never worked either
had arranged, and would share, a reward.

One put a bullet through a lung:
*That's for the times you got off!* –
*This is for Yugilbar sports day!*
Tom's wit drowned in his agonised cough.

As half of New England bewailed him,
diggers, carriers and Cobb and Co. men
with relations and not declared Bald Nob Hotel
black, in the new jargon of then.

I was thinking about New England,
of the Drummonds, the Wards and the Wrights,
how they'd all conjured gold from that country
by their different methods and lights.

All the gold I'd spun out of country
was imagery, remotely extolled,
but Tommy McPherson sported his with an air,
a black cousin with literal gold.

# The Cartoonist

Harry Reade, whom green students
called Harry the Bolshie
to his irritation,
argued with libertarians
and savagely with Hungarians
and recited Spanish verbs
while trolleying cadavers
in the School of Anatomy

in a fever to reach Cuba
and fight in the Revolution
since it had taken hold there.
Harry Reade spoke of camping
in hollow logs with his father –
then vanished for ten years
to the Bay of Pigs,
to cartooning for *¡Hoy!*

Che and Fidel called him
their kangaroo, their mascot,
but when he wept home
by ship up the Harbour
he'd also cartooned
in Toronto, on the *Star.*
The Revolution was fine
for getting parasites out

of the bloodstreams of children
but not for the mind,
the life of the mind,
Kangaroo Harry told me.

Ten more years, and he lived
at the Harold Park Hotel
by the dog track, the harness track –
the Harold Park, where poor teens
heard six poets for one beer –
Harry wrote plays for there,
one of Rudd, Steele, caricaturist
hustling a man to the gallows

and the Revolution, ay
¡la Revolucion! was all back,
Bay of Pigs and of Missiles
in its full santería.
Now his ashes would be scattered
on a park in la Habana,
Harry Reade, all alone
and in time it was done.

He led his kindly ash-bearers
past an enormous field
where a running man screamed
threats at them because a child
in their party chewed a cane-stub:
¡Yanquis, sabotajeando el azúcar!
But no, they were Australians,
un veterano, sus cenizas –

and Harry kept his course
in the week that Fidel
conceded his error
in having banned the Beatles.

## Manuscript Roundel

What did you see in the walnut?
Horses red-harnessed criss cross
and a soldier wearing the credits
of his movie like medal ribbons.
An egg in there building a buttery
held itself aloft in its hands –
red straps then pulled the nut shut.

I hope he stayed unrescued
as he wished to be
living out his mystery
in a hotel built too regal,
licensed, floor-hosed and legal,
to afford sailors and workmen
coming to with dunnage gone
on windjammers far at sea.

# Winding Up at the Bootmaker's

The widow handing out
her husband's last repair jobs,
each already newsprint-wrapped

sits meanwhile in their unlit shop
hands open in her lap.
Bitter grief has nearly smoothed her skin.

Kneeling up in Mediterranean black,
reaching down the numbered parcels
as if returning all their wedding gifts.

# Acknowledgements

Poems in this collection have appeared in the *Adelaide Review*, *Age*, *Alhambra Poetry Calendar 2008*, *Archipelago*, *Ars Interpres*, *Australian Literary Review*, *Commonweal*, *Crisis*, *Evansville Review*, *Edinburgh Review*, *First Things*, *Fiddlehead Review*, *Harvard Review*, *Image*, *Journal of Commonwealth Writing*, *Killing the Black Dog* (Black Inc.), *Lemuria* (India), *Liter*, *Little Star*, *London Review of Books*, *Manhattan Review*, *Matchbox*, *Meanjin*, *New Yorker*, *PN Review*, *Poetry Daily*, *Pratik* (Nepal), *Quadrant*, *Qualm*, *Poetry Oxford*, *Poetry Scotland*, *Rialto*, *Reader*, *Subtropics*, *The Show Is Not Over: 100 Years of Hopetoun Show* (White Crane Press), *Times Literary Supplement* and *Vallum*.